For:
Carlos ¡
Evangelina
from
your friend,

Enjoy! Anniel

Merry Christmas 2021!

Midnight Thoughts:

A Fusion of Poetry and Visual Arts

Author: Annick Lemay

Publisher: Rutherford Press
           https://rutherfordpress.ca

For information, contact:

           Rutherford Press,
           PO Box 648
           Qualicum Beach, BC, V9K 1A0, Canada
           info@rutherfordpress.ca

Printed in the United States of America and Canada

ISBN # 978-1-988739-41-0

cover art by Anita Lemay

layout by George Opacic

Contents

© Annick Lemay, 2018, *Kid bw,* photography

© Annick Lemay, 2018, *Inward Petal,* photography

Dedication

To my mother Anita, whose spirit sighs within me with every breath I take, my two

sons Etyel and Bryce, the greatest gifts Life has allowed me, my grandmother Andrée

and my father Lenic who taught me the love of the written word. Finally, to the

memory of my grandfather Jean-Paul Lemay, a better man I have yet to meet.

© Annick Lemay, 2019, *Blue Dancer,* pastels on canvas 24" x 36"

Intro Phrase

Muses dancing by my side...

To Love and Light and Words Alive!

© Annick Lemay, 2018, *Beach Cloud Sunset,* photography

Midnight Thoughts

There is a purpose to all things,

An Infinite Balance

That allows us

To appreciate its Opposite Experience,

That sheds Light on the meaning of Life

A Clue...

A first step to enlightenment and true happiness...

Without Illness,

We wouldn't appreciate Health

Without Sorrow

We wouldn't appreciate Happiness

Without Shadows and Darkness,

We wouldn't appreciate

Clarity and Truth...

Without Pain

We wouldn't appreciate our Magnificent Bodies

Without Discord and Conflict,

We wouldn't appreciate Peace...

Without the agonies of addiction

We wouldn't appreciate the Freedom from Obsession

Without poverty,

How are we to enjoy wealth?

Without greediness

What would become of generosity?

Without Reflection and Inner Search

We incapacitate ourselves

We close doors forever open

To our eyes and soul...

Reflection

That leads us to cultivate

Patience and understanding...

Without Surrendering

There is no possibility of Seeing

That everything is Perfect

All of the time...

That fighting the Universal Force

Is futile.

That sometimes we just need to get Battered

By Life's own Nature,

So that we can emerge in a Humble State

And finally know Peace...

That's how you get there;

That's the key to unlocking Wisdom

And higher Power...

The meaning of life is just that...

Enjoying the ride!

Accepting everything as it comes...

© Annick Lemay, 2018, *Train Tracks,* photography

And as you start to Feel

Its Palpability and inner Roar,

The Insistence of its Surf...

You become a Part Of It.

You share and Impart.

You naturally become

A Channel Of Its Light...

Quiet the mind...

Feel the Fear and do it anyway...

Know that you are never alone,

In this magnificent Journey,

This adventure called

Life...

© Annick Lemay, 2018, *Crane Water*, photography

A Word Too Many (or Alzheimer's)

Mother, you said a word too many

And now you've forgotten

All manner of speech.

You've decided

From this world,

To just walk away.

And I know

You just want to lose your way.

Decided from this world

To excuse yourself.

Dementia. Alzheimer's.

Who truly cares?

But please,

I solemnly swear

© Annick Lemay, 2018, *Lilac single,* photography

Word Too Many (or Alzheimer's)

That if you refrain

From slipping away

I vow to procure us

Many more adventures yet.

Oh, Mother,

Just will your strength

To build up again.

Leave some crumbs

To find your way back

From the Forest of your mind,

So that when I call,

You'll be ready and prepared

And into brilliant thresholds

Together we shall

Yet walk again.

I miss you so...

© Annick Lemay, 2018, *Infinite Dream*, photograph/mixed media

The Infinite Dream

To Dvorak, to Mahler

To my grandparents, to my mother,

To all dreams dreamt,

And waiting to be dreamt,

To the friend love.

To life reciprocate.

To all my dead

That I will never forget ...

To those who love me

To those who just pretend

To those who take care of me

To those who are content

To my beloved children

To those to whom I need to be explained,

Here I am, here I will remain...

To my friends

To my enemies

To what I know

To what I don't know

To those whom I leave without mention

Forgive me, my memory is no longer young

To my face lines,

Irrefutable proof that I have survived.

To this seductive planet

To the mysteries to come

To my enemies,

That from them I also learn.

To Bach, to the Brandenburgs,

To Hemingway, Steinbeck, and Austen,

To art, music, and literature.

To the human species.

To my dead, to my living,

To my family,

Of me, all a special part...

© Annick Lemay, 2019, *River Beach*, photography

To betrayal, to love

To lessons learnt

That overload my heart.

To Cabral, To Sosa, To Garcia-Marquez,

To Borges, To Kipling,

To Cervantes,

To Poetry...

My time on this planet,

But a poem in progress...

To know how to appreciate

To know how to love

To know how to forgive

To learn how to forget.

To my life, to my mind,

Scattered fragments lost in time...

To those who made me humble

To those who made me strong

To not be afraid to cry

To not be afraid to sing your song...

To my inner strength,

To my inner weakness,

To Rawat, To Kay, To Mozart, To Whitman,

To my body, to my mind

To my soul,

Essence of the spectacular ...

To those who saved my life,

To those who tried but to whom I did not listen to,

Forgive me, I have never been known for my intelligence ...

To clay,

That helps me create and grow

To those who care for me or just pretend.

To Borges, to Mahler,

To Mozart and Vivaldi.

To Kipling,

To Don Quixote, my beloved madness ...

To my ignorance,

To the beauty of more knowledge to come,

To this seductive planet,

To Death

On whom you can always count...

To Cousteau, to Sagan,

To the last moment,

To the last sigh,

To my wrinkles, sores and scars,

To my soul, heart, and body,

Irrefutable proof

That I have always fought.

To my art.

To the gift of being able to write.

To the passionate love

That to read I have.

© Annick Lemay, 2019, *Infinite Dream Face,* charcoals on art paper 11" x 17"

To the path to come,

To the abandoned road,

To the broken promise,

To the road too far left behind...

To risk

To losing, to winning

From everything I learn ...

To the child, who with infinite care

One must try to mold,

Clay perpetually drying,

A determined sculpture

One should strive for...

And after much walking, crying and thinking,

Life and its muses,

The call of the unknown...

© Annick Lemay, 2018, *Blue Crane Drawing, photography/mixed media* 12" x 16"

That's Just The Way It Goes

(song)

That's just the way it goes

We come alone,

We leave alone

People come and people go

Lovers Love

Haters Hate

Some Create

Some Destroy,

And some just

Couldn't care less...

There's the Noise Makers

They think it funny

When they force you

To walk in circular acres....

No matter

At the end of the day,

You walk alone

Leaving your footsteps

On the sand to be joined,

For a while,

By other footsteps

That required something from you

Or you required something from them

That's just the Universal Way...

Knowledge and experience interchanged.

On the Great Wide Shores,

The waves

Playfully erase

All footprints,

No matter their

Evolutionary Stage

If you look back

You can barely

Remember

Of lifetimes past...

When you look back

And see

How lots of footsteps

Joined yours

Some for a long while

Some for a short interval

Some were Masters

Some you taught

But the universe demands

An oh so healthy

Interchange...

A Balance.

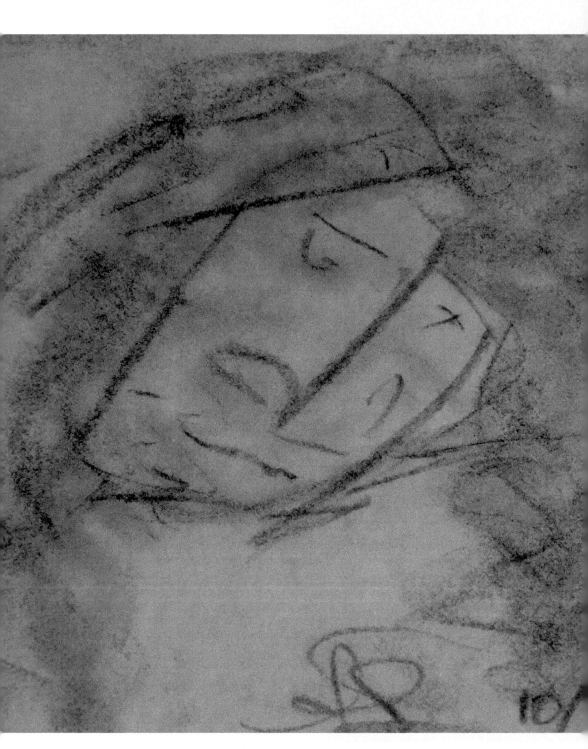

© Annick Lemay, 2013, *Blue Reggae,* pastels on canvas 24" x 36"

That's just the way it goes

We come alone

We leave alone

Evolution of the soul's

The name of the game

Or so they say,

I couldn't tell you

'Cause who am I

To judge right from wrong?

All I can say is

We come alone, we leave alone

And of some cries, crimes,

Towards our own

Sometimes is the universal way...

© Annick Lemay, 2018, *Blue Moon,* photography

A Mother's Prayer

Flesh of my flesh

Blood of my blood

I felt your first flutter

And then witnessed

Your first breath.

Saw your first Step

In what would become

The beginning

Of your walking away,

And engaging

In your own Sacred Path.

Powerless,

I could do naught

But wave;

© Annick Lemay, 2018, *To Write*, photography

And to the Moon pray

That,

In the darkest nights,

She'd always

Light your Path.

And so,

To the skies

I begged

You, to watch and protect;

Your gait follow

And allow you

Rise up

Whenever

You misstepped,

And when everything within you

Just wanted to falter or forget.

The Oceans

I then summoned

And asked

Your sailing

To oversee

While you travelled on its realms

To the winds

I asked

Gentle breeze

Guide your vessel,

Few tornadoes

Be allowed to pass

When you travelled

Under their watch

The Earth Goddess

I then Sought

Oh, Mother Of All Mothers

I pleaded

That you'd be able to recognize

The Power and Beauty in all Life.

To the Sun

I asked

To enter your Life

And your Heart

Always keep warm.

May you be allowed

To fall asleep

In Peace

At The end of your Life

To close your eyes

And Thank Them All

For a time well lived

© Annick Lemay, 2017, *Crane Pink Purple,* photography

To God

I then prayed

To always walk by your side

And gently wrap you

With the mysteries

Of Being Alive

And at The End

To the Heavens

I asked

To forever gently lead you

By the hand

© Annick Lemay, 2018, *Female Kayaker*, photography

T o y s

Toys. Really.

Things that are there

In that specific place

With the only purpose

But to please.

Because they're somehow important

They fill a certain

Specific void.

They feed a specific hunger

Like having

Watercolors, acrylics,

Pastels, oils.

Pen and paper

There.

Waiting.

To be instruments

Of inspiration

To fill yet another

Specific void.

The guitar,

But symbol

Of the muse of music in attendance.

The fireplace

The mirror

The lighting

The plants,

Some fake and some real

Just like me

They mirror

Me.

My son. Our little life together

A small camera

To fill the hunger to capture

The beauty of it all

A small, comfy,

Playful car

To save me from Pain

All there,

In my environment.

To fill

Voids.

To feed

Hungers.

To answer

Callings.

Different. All.

Specific to specific.

Moods and appetites,

Or Needs

To love or lose

Others or Myself...

My environment

Is created ultimately

To reflect me. Us.

I think I might even recognize

That I am

Loved

By my creator

Who, behind the scenes

Allows all this,

Helps create all this,

Helps facilitate

The Human Experience

And oh,

I thank you

So...

© Annick Lemay, 2017, *Fisherman,* photography

All is well

At the end

Of the day,

I feel loved,

I feel ok

Everything's at Peace

With the world

It was all worth it.

Thank you, God

Thank you Life,

Thank you All.

© Annick Lemay, 2018, *Fat Tree*, photography

In Life

In life

You

Must learn

When

To Bend

So you can Weather The Storms

Or

You Will Break...

© Annick Lemay, 2018, *Sea Otter,* photography

On Living

Living

Loving

Appreciation

Gratitude

Peace

Wonder

Learning

Teaching

Writing

Reading

Traveling

Painting

Photography

Creating

Patience

Forgiveness

Music

The Dance Of The Spheres

Meditation

To be in touch with Oneself

Friendship

Loyalty to Life, oneself, humanity

Balance

Proper alignment

Fairness

Health

Appreciation

Life

Plants

Animals

Aquariums

The sighing of the waves

The battling of the surf

The dying of the day.

La Côte Sauvage

Learning to heal oneself

And then maybe others

To be in touch

To summon positive energy within

And to others

Music

Awareness

Forests, jungles, beaches

Deserts.

Painting

Singing

Dancing

Writing

To be aware

Of your artistic needs

Of creating

Of what feeds you

Of your deepest longings

Of your gifts

Of your faults

To forgive oneself

And others

To let go...

Sculpture

Sailing

Riding

Driving

Astronomy

Photography

To be able to cry

To be able to laugh

To be able to rage

To be able to love

To be able

To go with the flow

To protect

And to be aware of how vulnerable

You really are

We really are

How life is so very precious

And oh god,

So very short

So...

Stop. Listen.

Your Heart is speaking

God is reaching

Creativity

Is always latent

So let go

Listen and appreciate

Your own, unique music

Once you are gone

Nothing will ever sound like you

© Annick Lemay, 2017, *Winter Tree*, photography

So give

Appreciate

Love

Let yourself be loved

Allow yourself

To Live

Love life

Living

Thinking

Giving

And yes,

Parting.

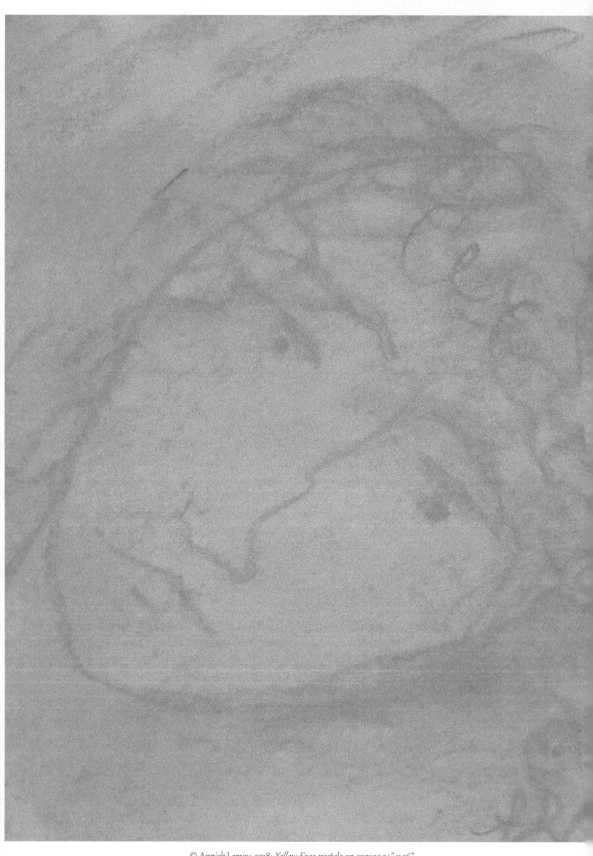

© Annick Lemay, 2018, *Yellow Face,* pastels on canvas 24" x 36"

On Loss

A void in space

You stare at something

That you know should be there,

Was there,

But just...

Is no more.

Vanished.

Few molecules remaining

As thoughts and memories,

No more

No whole.

Black hole in space.

Confusion.

Longing.

Deepest,

Excruciating,

Harrowing

Longing...

Exhaustion.

Oceans of regret

Trying to remember.

Deep uneasiness.

Sorrow.

Emptiness.

A child lost

That you were,

Just now

Holding by the hand.

An all-consuming

All-encompassing

Lack.

From air to breathe

To Inspiration.

The mind does not understand.

There is no trail

For it to follow Back.

And so the heart continues,

Dragging

Pleading

Arguing

Howling

Figuring

Puzzling

Crying

Wanting,

Remembering,

Piecing together,

Reviewing data,

No longer tangible.

No longer part of life

As can be recognized.

© Annick Lemay, 2018, *Mirror Clouds*, photography

Trying

To get

What's vanished

Back.

Trying to piece together

Deleted data

Lost in space.

Sorrow pounding,

Relentless,

Tireless,

Endlessly eroding,

Like the surf.

© Annick Lemay, 2019, *Crane all ocean vertical,* photography

On Truth

Truth doesn't come

In many colours,

Many shades

Of law

Of Universal Law.

Of feelings and cultures

Of history

Herstory.

Truth can never be dirtied

It can be insanely hard to take

Can and will decimate.

It displaces and replaces both.

Truth blinds with just one glimpse.

With just one flirty wink,

It can utterly destroy.

It can utterly create.

Truth is a favor of sight,

Of vision,

A gift.

Forces surrender.

To make way for its path.

Truth intimates also,

Softly in dreams at first,

And slowly to the front

Of the mind.

It kills without mercy

So that the unsustainable

Can finally fall,

Putrefy

And like everything else

Transform

Purify,

To birth something new

Not necessarily good nor pretty, nor noble

No.

Truth pays no tribute,

Makes no deals,

Holds no prisoners,

Does no favors.

It is evolution's right hand

It has no feeling, no emotion

Passes no judgement

Follows no script

Plays no games

Sees no games

Truth Is.

It forces Birth,

It invites Death.

Follows evolution.

It rips flesh and heart

Mind and spirit

Transforms matter

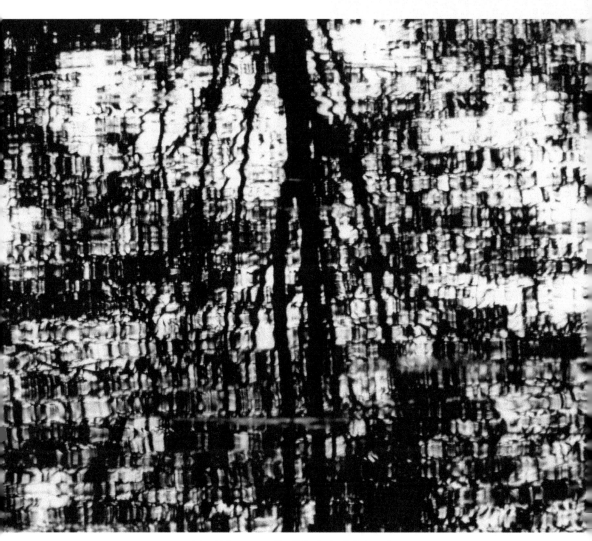

© Annick Lemay, 2019, *Tree Reflection Leaf,* photography

Ravages on its path;

So that it can emerge

As Is.

And exist.

Absolute.

Whole.

Clean.

Clear,

Pure Light.

Its interpretation and manipulation;

however,

Falls to mankind...

© Annick Lemay, 2018, *Sunset River,* photography

Little House or Five Elements

In my little house

There is

An aquarium

Waiting to be filled

To represent the ocean (water)

In my little house, there is a fire

To Remind us there is warmth in the World,

In my little house

There are plants

To represent

Mother Earth

In my little house

There is a bird

To represent volatility and air

In my little house

There are books

To represent Knowledge

In my little house

There is a son

To represent the magic of nature

And the power of love.

In my little house

There are art supplies

Pens and paper

To honor the muses

And their endless dance

In my little house

There is music

To help me

When I need to fall apart.

For the musician

The love for his violin

For the painter

The ecstasy of endless colors

For the poet

The drunkenness

Of Inspiration.

In my little house

I create quiet

To give me a chance

To sound my own heart and soul

All unconsciously

Most of the time

To fill the need

Of my own humanity

Anything to put me in touch

With the subtlety of the human experience.

To create an environment

That gives you a hint

The thread that connects you

With the deepest mysteries

To show you perhaps

How to fill your own heart

To expand

Your Understanding,

Your consciousness

© Annick Lemay, 2013, *Lies,* charcoal on paper 24" x 36"

And at the end

That leaves you with

An odd satisfaction of the heart

The thread that connects us

With the unknown

The filling of that thirst.

You know the one.

The One

That we run blindly

In all directions

To satisfy.

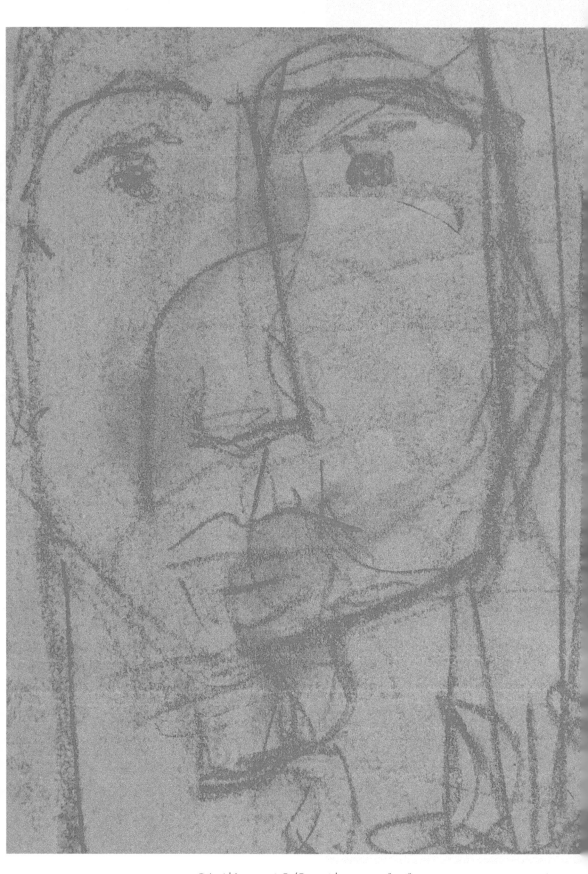

© Annick Lemay, 2018, *Red Face,* pastels on canvas 24" x 36"

The Herd

If you leave the herd

You are eaten by lions,

Then hyenas

Vultures disperse your bones

To the four winds,

You are told.

Law of the jungle.

Expected to blindly obey.

Make sure then,

To pack with you,

Friends.

Sorry,

I don't need to think

Before I convey

That

Without explanation

I can't fulfill anyone's expectation

© Annick Lemay, 2019, *Kayakers Right Cool,* photography

Environment

If your environment

Reflects

Your inner life,

If all is everywhere

But you know where everything is,

If You surround yourself

With music,

Books, colors,

Myriad

Operating systems,

Whichever

Tools you need

To facilitate

To Experience

That which feeds you.

If books, notebooks, and pens

Are your companions,

Beloved friends,

Always at the ready

To take

Whatever it is that makes you

Feel alive,

That help you translate your message,

Your gift,

Like a loyal army,

Your tools do not contest,

At the ready

They stand,

To give unconditional acceptance

To any and all,

Feelings, thoughts,

Creations or garbage...

If you have

One human being

That you can love

And be loved by,

If little creatures you have around,

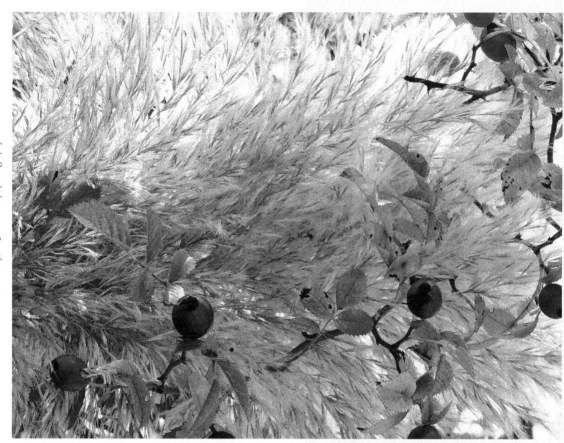

99

Ready to answer your call;

And reveal to you

The mysteries of unconditional love,

If you can wonder

About Inspiration,

Creation,

Desperation sometimes,

Divinity perhaps.

The muses dancing by your side...

If all these,

And your Will conspire

To keep you on your path

So that you can recognize

And live

The true love affair

That happens with your own self

When you open your consciousness

And realize

That you may have

Something to give,

Something to learn,

Something to receive...

And when you perceive

The inner You,

You can't but wonder

At how loyal

And true,

How revealing,

Disclosing,

Engaging,

Embracing,

Decimating,

Disturbing at times,

Your inner-self truly is.

Facilitating creativity,

Revelations.

A unique relationship

It truly is.

A truly honorable love-affair...

© Annick Lemay, 2019, *River Cool Hwy,* photography

And when distractions

Keep banging,

Piercing,

Pulling,

Trying to displace

That focus,

Try to maintain it

Impenetrable.

Your awareness

Helps birth

The ensuing lesson-creation,

The moment too precious, fleeting,

A gift well meant.

A Life's moment interpretation.

Why not

Pay attention,

At the end of the day,

There is only One Life,

Only One Me.

Only one You.

Only one Us.

Only One Humanity.

© Annick Lemay, 2018, *Hummingbird,* photography

Waking Up

A Fire,

The Mellow Light,

A Remembrance

Of The One

I Love;

A Higher State

Of Consciousness,

A Focus On Inbreath.

Waking Up,

Deep In Space,

Dancing Slowly

The dance

Of The Spheres

Waking Up,

Drunk With Gratitude

To Be One Of The Chosen Ones

To be A Dancer Tonight

To be a dancer in this lifetime

God, How Long Has it Been?

The Slow Breathing

Of My Sleeping Child

His Kisses

His Feeling Safer

For Now

The Soft Murmur

Of Life,

A Storm Outside

Claims Water And Air,

Electricity

When I Finalize with The Earth

For Tonight.

© Annick Lemay, 2019, *Sunflowers*, photography

Waking Up

To Knowing.

To Knowledge.

The perfect conduit;

That It's

Time To Share

The lessons

So expensively

Learnt.

© Annick Lemay, 2018, *Pink Mushrooms,* photography

Pour Anthony Bourdain

Antoine des trois étoiles

Antoine des quatre étoiles

Antoine, enfin des cinq étoiles

Étoiles qui ont fini par dégoûter

Au lieu d'une passion

Cela s'est transformé en boulot

Et comme tout boulot

Qui a déjà dégoûté

Tu as voulu changer

M ais de cet endroit enchanté

In n'y avait pas d'endroit abrité

De la multitude

D'ombres envisagées

À la planète tu as dit: "non"

Et pas non plus

À la vie parmi nous

Tu as décidé, dans les cieux

D'aller t'abriter,

© Annick Lemay, 2018, *Blue Stars,* photography/mixed media

Ne pouvant plus aimer

Au zéphyr du cosmos tu t'y es ajouté

Je te reverrai bientôt

Frère bien-aimé

Et on ira bouffer avec les copains

Pour toute éternité.

© Annick Lemay, 2018, *Flower Petal Inward part two*, photography

Que de Pouvoir S'Ouvrir

Que de pouvoir s'aimer

De pouvoir s'ouvrir

Un chemin

Laisser passer

Un autre

Être humain

Regarder

Admirer

Convoiter

Décifrer

Un nouveau chemin

En soi.

Développer.

Vouloir enfin rentrer

Chez soi.

On m'a appelée,

Aimée, tirée, poussée,

Bouleversée,

Sans doute pour pouvoir...

Quoi?

M'apprivoiser?

Vouloir continuer...

S'appaiser.

S'améliorer.

S'amplifier.

Se laisser aller.

S'empoter.

S'emporter.

S'envoler.

S'endommager

Se dédommager.

À la fin

Se dire merci

Et merci aussi

Aux autres qui ont

Tout facilité.

Pour ensemble

Protéger,

Veiller

Accompagner

Améliorer ...

Et dans la paix,

Enfin pouvoir

S'envoûter,

S'enchanter,

Se fasciner...

De ne jamais se laisser

Dompter.

Domestiquer.

S'alourdir.

Ne pas s'abasourdir

De lire

Le même livre.

La même histoire.

La même fin.

Attendre

Ne plus savoir ni qui,

Ni quoi,

Ni pourquoi.

Oublier.

Essayer de se débarrasser

Des chapitres passés.

D'essayer

De se rencontrer

De se redessiner

De se ré-inventer

De se re-designer

De se redeviner.

S'embrasser

Se soutenir

Dans cette vie,

Côte Sauvage

Mer enragée...

Soutenir,

Les autres,

Les siens,

Même sans espoir

Ne pouvoir

Bien regarder,

Ni supporter,

Les jours interminables.

Pourris parfois.

Malsains.

Ne pouvoir se défaire

S'en défaire,

D'essayer

De s'en moquer,

De toujours continuer

De marcher,

De courir,

De soutenir,

De, enfin,

Devenir...

De cacher son être

© Annick Lemay, 2019, *Tulip,* photography

Pour

Ne pas se laisser

Bousculer.

Emmerder.

Décoller.

Apprivoiser.

Basculer.

De continuer

À chercher

L'être entrevu.

Deviné.

Le bien de s'exprimer.

Le bien de s'expliquer.

De se comprendre.

Et d'ainsi

Finalement s'accepter,

S'accomplir, se réaliser.

Peut-être même

Pour ainsi dire,

S'aimer...

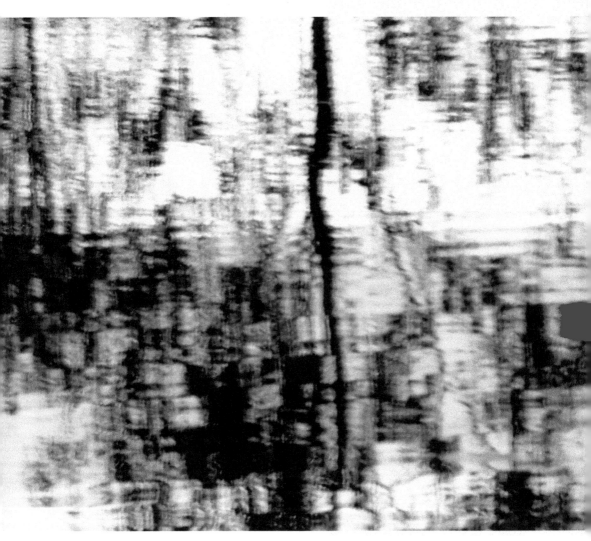

© Annick Lemay, 2018, *Tree Reflection H2O no leaf,* photography/mixed media

Plaisirs

Le plaisir de se dire

Qu'on a le droit de s'épanouir.

De créer.

De Lire.

D'écrire.

De composer.

De s'exprimer

Afin de pouvoir

Se sauvegarder ...

Afin de devenir

Un être

Un peu plus

Complet.

En sachant qu'on sera toujours

Des êtres inachevés.

De s'abstenir d'appartenir.

De consentir

À aimer et être aimé,

Sans pour autant

Se sacrifier.

De maintenir

Son équilibre.

D'éviter le trépas,

Le viol

Du Soi.

De garder,

Protéger,

Soigner,

Conserver...

D'étreindre

Son hémisphère.

De vouloir s'ajouter.

Se laissant le choix,

Toujours la possibilité,

De pouvoir s'excuser

Si le Soi est en danger.

En ayant toujours

© Annick Lemay, 2017, *Kickass Sunset lol*, photography

La certitude

D'un propos,

D'un destin,

D'un chemin inachevé,

D'une leçon

À commencer,

D'une leçon

À recommencer,

Jusqu'à ce qu'elle soit

Absorbée.

Assimilée.

Intégrée.

Afin qu'elle fasse partie

D'un être plus complet.

Plus comblé.

Mieux préparé...

Pouvoir,

Sur le prochain sentier,

S'embarquer;

Afin d'une vie plus riche

Achèver.

Sa vie

Respecter.

Imaginer.

Combler.

Développer.

Pardonner.

Apprécier.

Car la race humaine,

Et notre Mère-Terre,

Ont besoin

D'êtres mieux développés.

© Annick Lemay, 2018, *Tree Painting*, photography/mixed media 12" x 18"

Le Livre De Ma Vie

De se voir, de se revoir

De se dire et de se redire

D'essayer de s'épanouir...

De tourner la page

Du livre de sa vie

Témoin

De déjà trop

De chapitres vécus.

Livre,

Qui colle au mains.

Pages,

Qui coulent entre les doigts.

Chapitres,

Qui continuent à se débattre,

À écouter, à guetter,

À essayer de deviner,

Le mystère transpercer...

D'essayer de s'additionner,

Trop tôt,

À mon livre

Le livre de ma vie...

De lire, de voir

Une histoire déjà

Vue, lue

Revue, relue, revécue

Et déjà trop de fois

Ressentie....

La même leçon

Subodorée...

De vouloir ne plus lui dire au revoir

Mais adieu.

De vouloir abandonner

Au vent,

Ces derniers chapitres

Gauches,

Meurtris,

Déchirés,

Angoissés,

Affolés,

Malodorants.

© Annick Lemay, 2019, *Desert Mountain*, photography

Voulant désespérément

Les abandonner.

Pour pouvoir finalement

Le couplet accepter

Le poème assimiler.

Le récit achever.

La vie continuer,

Pouvoir respirer,

Pouvoir soupirer...

Afin que

Tout cela puisse

Se traduire

En calme, paix et sérénité...

Épreuves crevantes

Qu'on peût utiliser

Pour autrui,

Sur un autre chemin

Accompagner.

Pour essayer d'aider,

À traverser.

Faciliter

À rencontrer, à retrouver

L'Ancien Chemin;

Celui pour lequel on est destinés

Et qu'on n'aurait jamais dû

Abandonner.

Accident de trop de larmes

Pas toujours coulées,

De haine, de désespoir

Mal éprouvés,

De peurs, pas apprivoisées

D'amours, pas oubliés

De haines, mal interprétées

De leçons, mal assimilées.

De larmes jamais déversées...

Histoire d'essayer d'oublier,

Qu'envers la vie,

Il existe une responsabilité.

Assimiler

Que toute épreuve

A pour but

Qu'un nouveau Soi

Exigerait-il d'être né.

Et qu'au moment

D'accoucher,

Cet être nouveau,

Finalement visible,

Je ne veux

Que combler,

Qu'ajouter,

Qu'embrasser,

Et Remercier...

(Je ressens comme la vie

M'a accordé un arrangement,

Un entendement,

De pouvoir tourner la page,

Pour pouvoir lui faire la place,

© Annick Lemay, 2018, *Little Girl bw,* photography

Et faire partie

Dans un nouveau chapitre

De ce livre de ma vie.

Un nouvel être

Qu'on croît de loin,

Peut-être même bien,

Reconnaître...

J'espère

L'apercevoir de loin.

Je l'attends avec terreur et impatience.

Une fenêtre de rennaissance

Une fenêtre de reconnaissance,

Une fenêtre, enfin, de connaissance...

Et au moment de l'accouchage

Je vois déjà

Un beau sourire épanoui,

Alors je cours à sa rencontre,

Nouveau chapitre

Dans ce livre de ma vie...

© Annick Lemay, 2017, *Sunset River*, photography

To Reading (Tool)

Lifelong companion

In times of peace and war.

Loyal, like writing,

Best friend.

Loyal dog.

Unconditional

Lifesaver.

Tool to think

Tool to lose yourself into

Tool to address your innermost feelings

Tool to sleep while awake

Tool to be awake while asleep

Tool to be alive in death

Tool to be dead in life

Tool to laugh

Tool to cry

Tool to escape

Tool to confront

Tool to lose yourself

Tool to find yourself again

Key to worldly knowledge

Tool to penetrate

Tool to be part of

Tool to ascend

Tool to descend

Tool to walk other's paths

Tool to feel other's hearts

Tool to feel older's hearts

Tool to experience

Tool to taste

Tool to visit other's realms

Tool to figure out

Tool to plan

In silence

Tool to digest

Tool to muse and ponder

Tool to absorb

Tool to dance two paths and more.

© Annick Lemay, 2019, *Benevolent Skies,* photography

To Write

The inspiration muse,

The fluttering,

Tingling,

Otherworldliness...

Higher consciousness

Perhaps.

A little madness

A foot here, another someplace else.

It opens a flood

A torrential flood really

Of,

I don't know what

I can't stop

It feeds my essence

A cry of the soul

It allows me

To fulfill

The purpose of my existence.

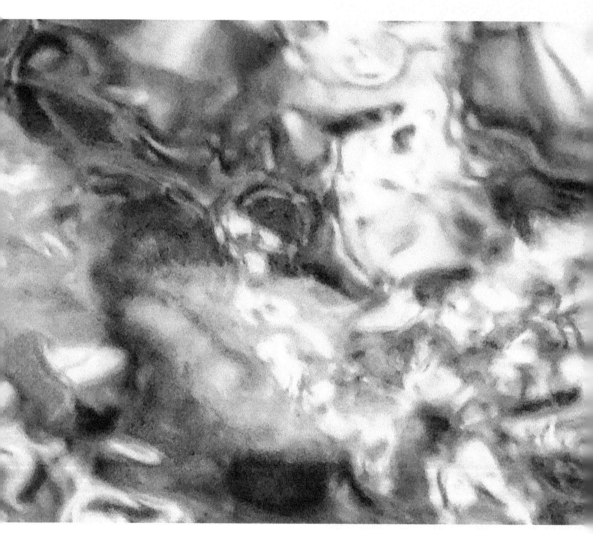

© Annick Lemay, 2018, *Babby's H2O*, photography

It touches

Deep. Inside.

And makes me feel whole

Puts me in touch.

I love to write

About the recognition

Of Life

The absolute beauty,

My very own

Ultimate connection

With Creation

With God

With the universe

That I carry

That carries me,

Of which I am

But a drop of dust

In a milky way.

A drop in the ocean

Conveying

With incredible certitude

That it is where I belong

It puts me in the flow

With the essence of life

Or so it feels,

Just right.

It is so mysterious

So deep,

So capricious

That my humble pen

Cannot ever be deserving.

Just a mere speculation

A fluctuation,

The heartbeat of my life

Can maybe give justification,

© Annick Lemay, 2019, *Sunset River Cool*, photography

An interpretation

An explanation

Mere speculation

Of why I need to write

It is what was bestowed upon me

At my conception

And for better or for worse

My calling.

My means of transportation

So capricious

An affectation.

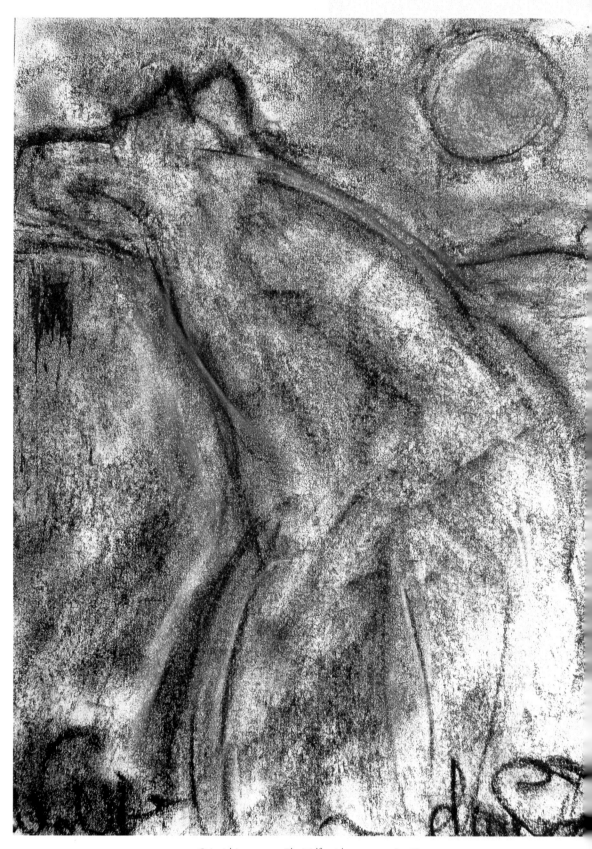

© Annick Lemay, 2017, *Blue Wolf*, pastels on canvas 24" x 36"

Dear Anyone

Be brave, but quiet

Be handsome, but hidden

Be vociferous, but silent

Be grateful.

Be wise, but know nothing

Keep walking, getting to your destination

Love them

But don't let them know

Be Loyal

But never be surprised

When you feel the blade

Sink between your shoulders

Cry.

But don't let them see

(They feed on it, you see)

Journey without hurry

Get Home,

No doubt.

© Annick Lemay, 2019, *Crane Go Getter*, photography/mixed media 24" x 36"

The Question

The question is not

Whether someone loves you

But whether you're going to allow

Yourself to be loved.

The question lies not

In whether somebody

Trusts you

But whether you'll allow

To trust anyone too,

(And whether you'll ultimately believe it)

After so much betrayal.

The question doesn't lie

In whether you can forgive

But whether you will forgive

Under certain circumstances

The question doesn't lie

In whether you can be forgotten

But whether you'll be able to ever forget.

The question doesn't lie

In whether you can be believed

But whether the other person

Will have the courage

To believe you

And in you.

The question lies not

In whether you can get yourself

To open again

It lies in whether you'll force yourself

To believe in the game

Yet again...

© Annick Lemay, 2018, *Pissed Off Clouds,* photography

If

If you have no Honour

If you use the Weak

The desperate, the hungry

And the Beaten Soldiers

Coming back from war

If your festivities lie in craving

Someone else's blood, sweat and tears

If you use gassed children

And exhausted,

Desperate mothers

To sustain you,

If you have no laws

To keep you

Despised from the rest of the jungle

You shall always be

Not worthy of Anyone

Or Anything

Anywhere,

At anytime

Or to be paid

Any real mind,

Except as a social study

A guinea pig

In a laboratory.

© Annick Lemay, 2018, *Baby Eagle*, photography

How Can You

How can you learn

When you weren't taught to observe?

How can you listen

When you weren't taught to hear?

How can you look

When you weren't taught to discern?

How can you touch

When you weren't taught

What's safe?

How can you communicate

When you weren't taught to enunciate?

How can you trust

When all you were taught is deceit?

How can you love

If all you've learnt

Is how much it can hurt

In the aftermath

No wonder

You just won't open your eyes.

© Annick Lemay, 2019, *Kip To Print,* photography

Just Guessing or To Dogs

I guess one of the things

I cannot

Must not

Refute

Is that I need to Love.

Love anything, anyone

I'm not picky

A fish, a plant, a book.

Preferably,

A child, a man, a dog.

To non-conditional

I always aim;

But as a human

I must concede

That the only unconditional love

Comes from a dog.

So,

With all candor I must say

That I'll do my very best.

Someone who will hold my hand

And if I'm to soar up into the Skies

Or drown into the seas

Will soar or drown

And never let go of my hand...

© Annick Lemay, 2018, *Black Crayola Pansies,* photography/mixed media 24"x 36"

Communication

People sometimes

Deliver communications

According to their interpretation

It's up to you

To change

The translation,

To subdue the interpretation,

To ignore the

Misrepresentation

To translate

The Interpretation.

© Annick Lemay, 2019, *Wave Splash Fav Song part 1*, photography

My Favorite Song

My favorite songs you ask...

Let me think...

Life is my favorite song.

Love,

Generosity of spirit.

Wisdom.

Knowledge.

Wellness.

Health.

Children's laughter.

Tears.

Sorrow, and then its absence.

The Human Race.

To recognize the need for imbalance...

To Live each day

As if it was your last.

Evolution.

The contact and awareness of it.

The lack of it....

TREMORS, FEAR, HATE;

AND THEIR CONQUEST.

Uncertainty.

Music...

The Dance Of The Spheres....

The palpability of the human experience.

Courage.

Nobility of the Soul.

FORGIVENESS.

The need to love unconditionally.

The flow of life and its waves.

The ocean of experiences.

Feelings Hated,

Feelings acknowledged. Respected.

© Annick Lemay, 2019, *Wave Splash Fav Song part 2,* photography

And finally Accepted.

To Enrich if possible.

My favorite song you ask?

Why, the ability to experience the adventure!

The ability to enamor yourself with yourself!

And then,

To give the possibility away...

To Give It Away.

That is my favorite song...

Being Able To Give It Away....

© Annick Lemay, 2018, *Book Close-up*, photography

© Annick Lemay, 2019, *Photographer Far*, photography

This Notebook

This notebook is done

The story is finished

This cycle completed

There are no more pages

I care to put pen to paper on

There will be more pages

White, clear, clean

For someone else

To fill.

© Annick Lemay, 2018, *Kid End.* photography

Parting Words

With Love

And Light

To you,

My parting words are.

Try and

Be happy

With who you are.

Blessings,

Annick Lemay

© Annick Lemay, 2018, *Author Self Portrait,* photography

List of Illustrations

Thank you kindly for reading this book

If you wish to see the author's

page on Rutherford Press

and perhaps leave a comment

please check it out here:

https://rutherfordpress.ca/annick-lemay/

For information on the

author's art and photography

please visit:

https://annicklemayartsand-photography.com/

CPSIA information can be obtained
at www.ICGtesting.com
Printed in the USA
BVHW022241180521
607589BV00002B/13